Lost and Found Cat

The True Story of Kunkush's Incredible Journey

Doug Kuntz and Amy Shrodes

Illustrated by **Sue Cornelison**

Crown Books for Young Readers

New York

Late one night in August 2015, a car driven by a smuggler snuck out of the city of Mosul, in the country of Iraq. The smuggler's passengers were a mother and her four daughters and one son.

Their father had recently died.
Sura, the mother, had paid the smugglers to help her
family flee the country. Mosul had become too dangerous

A few days earlier, the family had gotten ready to leave. Since they could only bring what they could carry, they had packed just one bag full of food and water. They would buy clothes later. But Sura had decided they could not leave without their beloved cat, Kunkush (KUN-koosh). Sura prayed that the cat, hidden in a small carrier, would stay quiet. If the smuggler discovered Kunkush, he would make her pay a great deal more money.

Two hours later, the car stopped and they were told to get out.
Another smuggler met them and led them on foot through forests
and over mountains, stopping only to eat and sleep in the woods.
Sura feared for her children—Rihab (18), Hakam (16), Maab (11),
Ahab (10), and Ansab (9). But they saw it as an adventure, often
singing as they walked during the three-day journey.

Sura and her son, Hakam, took turns carrying Kunkush at the back of the line, so that if the cat meowed, the smuggler would not hear him. Whenever they stopped to rest, Sura took Kunkush behind some trees to let him out and feed him.

On the fourth day, they reached a Kurdish village, where another smuggler was waiting to take them to Istanbul, Turkey, in a bus. While the smuggler drove, the family had to be on the lookout for the patrols trying to catch them.

The family stayed in the city for two weeks, moving from one apartment to another. At least Kunkush could wander freely inside.

Finally, it was time to cross the Aegean Sea to Greece.
The family boarded another bus and drove to a place called
Izmir, on the Turkish coast. Then they walked three hours
along the beach, until they were told to put on life jackets.

The Greek island of Lesbos was six miles across the water. Kunkush and his family were crammed aboard a flimsy rubber boat. It was meant to carry only twenty-five people, but there were more than sixty men, women, and children on the boat. Plus one secret cat.

Almost as soon as the overcrowded boat launched, it began taking on water because it was too heavy. From the shore, people shouted at the passengers to throw their belongings overboard to make the boat lighter, but most refused. Sura tried to hold Kunkush's carrier above the water, until a wave drenched them all.

The sinking boat had to return to shore. As a crush of people got off, Kunkush's carrier door was broken. Determined to make the crossing, Sura told her kids to stay aboard.

The boat launched again, this time with fewer passengers. Sura was scared because only her son, Hakam, could swim. But her daughters were unconcerned, enjoying the ride in the sun after weeks of hiding. The three-hour crossing to Lesbos felt like it flew by thanks to their excitement.

Volunteers in Greece waited on the shore to help the hundreds of refugees arriving every day. As soon as the boat reached the beach, panicky, shivering passengers scrambled to get off. Hakam splashed ashore with Kunkush and put the carrier on dry land. Then he hurried back to help his mother off the boat.

Wet and frightened, Kunkush pushed his way out of the broken
door of his carrier. He quickly disappeared into the forest like a deer.

While the rest of the boat passengers were loaded onto a bus to continue their journey, the family refused to leave without their cat. Several volunteers helped them look for Kunkush. They searched for hours.

At last they had to give up. The heartbroken family needed to leave, taking the next step toward their new home.

In a little fishing village on Lesbos, near where Kunkush's family had arrived, there lived a colony of island cats. No one owned them, but fishermen kept them well fed.

A few days after Kunkush's family had left, volunteers noticed
a white cat hanging around the local cafés. The white cat's fur
was filthy and matted. He looked like he was starving.

The local cats seemed to know he was a stranger. They hissed
and spat and chased him away.

One of the volunteers, Amy, told her friend and fellow volunteer, Ashley, about the cat she'd seen. Could this white cat be the one the family had lost? After questioning villagers and searching the island, Amy and Ashley found the white cat and took him to a local vet.

Dr. Konstantina shaved the cat's matted, filthy fur. She gave him his shots and other medicines. But this cat needed a name for now. Dr. Konstantina suggested Dias, to give him strength. Dias is the Greek name for Zeus, the king of the ancient Greek gods.

The friends took Dias back to Amy's apartment. His shaved fur was still full of sand and bugs. Amy bathed and scrubbed him until he was clean.

Five minutes after his bath, the exhausted cat collapsed facedown, mid-meow, and slept.

Dias stayed with Amy for over a month. Often he prowled around her
apartment, yowling loudly. Amy believed he was looking for his family.

Reunite Dias

Please click **HERE**
to donate.

Amy and her friends were determined to reunite Dias with his family. But where were they? Volunteers created flyers, and Amy's friend Michelle back in the United States made a Facebook page for him. People contributed money to help pay for his medical care and travel. Before long, news stories about the lost cat appeared around the world. Millions of people saw the videos, articles, and Facebook updates about Dias. He had become famous.

Amy was fairly sure that Dias's family had left Greece. Many of the refugee families had traveled to Germany. Since Amy's time in Lesbos was ending, she made plans to take Dias to Germany. She and Dias flew to Berlin, where a British couple named Emma and Simon had agreed to take care of him and continue the search. If his family could not be found after a year, they would adopt him.

And then, on Valentine's Day, the family saw their lost cat on a news website. The oldest daughter, Rihab, who had learned some English, contacted Amy and her friends through Facebook. Everyone had been looking in the wrong place! The family was living in Norway, not Germany. Rihab told Amy that Dias's real name was Kunkush.

The volunteers arranged a Skype visit. When the family saw the fluffy white cat on the screen, they called "Kunkush!" His ears perked up. He started searching for his family.

A photographer named Doug, in Lesbos and Germany to show the refugees' story to the world, agreed to fly with Kunkush from Germany to Norway. But when he got to the airport in Berlin, the supervisor behind the counter told him he could not board the plane.

"That carrier is too small," she said with a sniff.

By this time, a crowd had gathered around Doug and his yowling white cat. Doug pleaded with her. He told her the carrier was the right size.

"That carrier is so small, the cat cannot turn around," she snapped.

At that moment, Kunkush made a dramatic 180-degree turn inside his carrier. The crowd laughed, and the supervisor grudgingly agreed to allow them onto the plane.

In Norway, Doug rented a car and drove two hours to the family's new home. They were waiting eagerly for him. So was a team of camerapeople and reporters.

Sura opened the door and blinked at the bright lights of the cameras. Then she burst into tears as Doug placed Kunkush in her arms. *"Ma habibi!"* she murmured. That's Arabic for "my darling." The entire family crowded around their long-lost pet.

After four months and thousands of miles, Kunkush and his family were finally together in their new home. "We are all safe now," said Sura.

A Note from Doug and Amy

When we first met Kunkush, we knew that he must have been very special to someone. Imagine how much his family loved Kunkush to carry him out of a war zone.

Kunkush reminded us of our pet friends back home, and how we would feel if we lost them because of war or a natural disaster. What wouldn't we give to see them again?

This is why we knew we had to try to find his family. The search wasn't easy. People in many different countries banded together, working for months until finally the seemingly impossible was achieved. Kunkush's family was found in Norway—and we were able to reunite them!

The refugee crisis is one of the most monumental events happening in our world today. Millions of people have fled countries like Syria, Afghanistan, Iraq, and parts of Africa seeking a safer life. We both went to Greece because we felt compelled to help, each in our own way—Amy as a volunteer helping the arriving refugees, and Doug as a photojournalist, bringing the plight of the refugees to people around the globe.

We are living in a unique time in history, a time when the Internet allows us to meet people from other cultures and hear their perspectives about what is going on in our world. We all have something valuable to share and the ability to reach out and help. This story is about making that choice. It is only because of all the people who got involved that Kunkush found his family. His story helps us remember that we all need each other.

On May 20, 2016, Kunkush passed away suddenly from a feline virus. He was surrounded by his loving family. While we wish his life could have been longer, he left this world knowing that he was loved unconditionally. This book is his legacy, bringing hope to others through his story.

A portion of the proceeds from this book will go toward lifting up more people around the world.

Doug Kuntz and Amy Shrodes

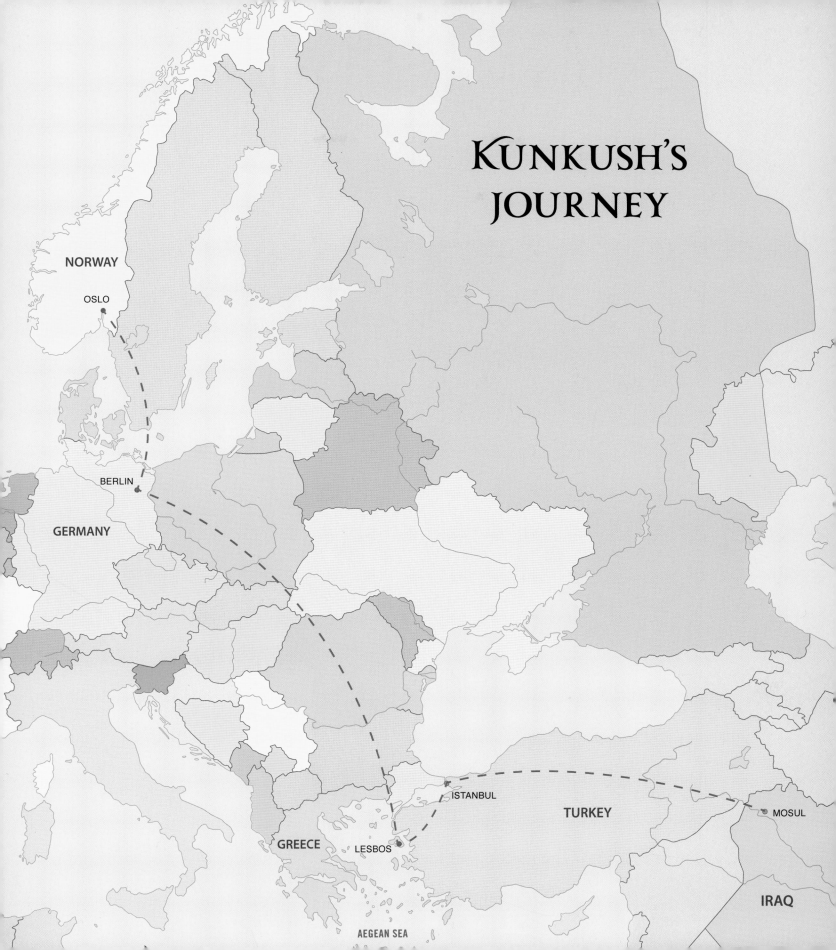

KUNKUSH'S JOURNEY

NORWAY

OSLO

BERLIN

GERMANY

GREECE   LESBOS

İSTANBUL

TURKEY   MOSUL

IRAQ

AEGEAN SEA

A Remarkable Journey

Boat landings on Lesbos are chaotic as volunteers like Amy help guide the boats to shore in the rough surf.

Like Sura and her children, these Muslim families have left their war-torn countries seeking safety in Europe.

Kunkush finally found his way to this community of wild cats, but they wouldn't let him join their group.

By the time Amy and Ashley found Kunkush, he had been through very rough times.

Kunkush, skinny and shaved, waits for his family to find him.

Amy took good care of Kunkush in Greece, until a foster family was found in Germany.

Kunkush and his passport are ready
for the trip to Germany.

Sura was overcome with emotion
when she was reunited with Kunkush.

Sura and Kunkush were so happy to
be together again in their new home
in Norway.